THE UNCLE BEN'S HEALTHY EATING COOKBOOK

SMITHMARK

INTRODUCTION

Nutrition Experts Say We Need To Eat Healthier

Nutrition experts tell us we can live longer, healthier lives if we change the way we eat. Typically, about 40% of the calories in the American diet come from fat, 45% from carbohydrates and 15% from protein. Both the USDA and the National Research Council on Diet and Health now recommend that we increase the amount of carbohydrates we eat to 55% of our daily calories and limit fat consumption to no more than 30%.

UNCLE BEN'S® Brand Rice Can Help You To Eat Healthier

Versatile UNCLE BEN'S® Brand Rice is an important part of a healthier diet. An excellent source of energy-giving complex carbohydrates, it contains no cholesterol, virtually no fat or sodium, and provides only about 90 calories per satisfying half-cup serving. In addition UNCLE BEN'S® Original and Fast Cooking Brown Rices are natural sources of dietary fiber and rice bran.

Take A Healthy Eating Tip From Our U.S. Olympic Athletes

U.S. Olympic athletes, trainers and coaches know that eating right gives them a winning edge . . . and that rice is an important part of healthy eating. That's why UNCLE BEN'S® Brand Rice, the highest quality rice available, has been served daily at the U.S. Olympic Training Centers for years. UNCLE BEN'S® Brand Rice can give you and your family the same winning edge in your move toward a healthier diet.

Healthy Eating Can Be Easy

The recipes in this cookbook were specially created to make healthy eating enjoyable and easy. Each recipe conforms to the USDA dietary recommendations by providing a high percentage of calories from complex carbohydrates and 30% or fewer calories from fat. Sodium levels also are carefully controlled. Main dishes contain less than 730mg of sodium per serving (⅓ of the USDA recommended daily intake of sodium); side dishes and desserts contain less than 365mg per serving.

If you are following a diet prescribed by a physician, consult a registered dietician to see how they can fit into your specific meal plans.

We hope you enjoy seeing for yourself how easy and delicious healthy eating can be with UNCLE BEN'S® Brand Rice and these great-tasting recipes.

UNCLE BEN'S® Brand Rice:
Official sponsor of the 1992 Olympic Games . . .
. . . and champion of healthy eating for everyone.

CLB 2598
©1992 Colour Library Books Ltd, Godalming, Surrey, England.
© Recipes Uncle Ben's Inc. 1992
All rights reserved.
This edition published in 1992 by
SMITHMARK Publishers Inc., 112 Madison Avenue, New York, NY 10016
Printed and bound in Singapore.
ISBN 0 8317 3193 1

SMITHMARK books are available for bulk sales promotion and premium use. For details write
or telephone the Manager of Special Sales, SMITHMARK Publishers Inc.,
112 Madison Avenue, New York, NY 10016. (212) 532-6600.

CREAMY CARROT SOUP

Serves 8

From the most finicky eater to the most sophisticated guest, everyone will be amazed at the creamy richness of this healthy soup.

1½ cups chopped onions
4 carrots, sliced
1 clove garlic, minced
½ tsp ground black pepper
⅛ tsp ground nutmeg
2 tbsps margarine
6 cups chicken broth
¾ cup UNCLE BEN'S® CONVERTED® Brand Rice
¾ cup whole milk
Shredded carrot and fresh chervil to garnish

---

1. In a stock pot, sauté onions, carrots, garlic, pepper and nutmeg in margarine for 1 minute over medium heat.

STEP 1

2. Add broth and rice. Bring to a boil, cover, reduce heat and simmer until the carrots and rice are tender – about 30 minutes.

STEP 2

3. Remove from heat. Carefully fill a blender container with half of the cooked vegetable and rice mixture and blend into a smooth purée. Pour purée into another pot and repeat purée procedure with remaining vegetable rice mixture.

STEP 3

4. When all the mixture has been puréed, stir in the milk and heat to just a simmer. Garnish with a small amount of shredded carrot and fresh chervil before serving.

Cook's Notes

t TIME: Preparation takes 10-15 minutes, cooking takes 35 minutes.

n NUTRITIONAL DATA PER SERVING:
Calories   160
Protein   7g
Carbohydrates   22g
Fat   5g (28% of Calories)
Sodium   600mg

MANHATTAN FISH CHOWDER

Serves 8

This zesty soup will warm the crowd without much effort from the cook.

4 cups vegetable juice cocktail
2 large tomatoes, chopped
1 cup chopped onion
1 large green bell pepper, chopped
4 large garlic cloves, minced
2 tsps lemon juice
2⅔ cups water
1 tsp dried basil, crushed
½ tsp dried oregano, crushed
1⅓ cups UNCLE BEN'S® CONVERTED® Brand
    Rice
½ tsp salt
¼ tsp ground black pepper
1lb flounder or sole fillets, skinned, cut into
    bite-sized chunks
Fresh basil to garnish

1. Combine vegetable juice cocktail, tomatoes, onion, green bell pepper, garlic, lemon juice, water, basil, oregano, rice, salt and pepper in a stock pot.

2. Bring to a boil, reduce heat and simmer, uncovered, for 15 minutes.

STEP 2

3. Add fish chunks and continue simmering until the fish flakes with a fork – approximately 5 minutes. Serve garnished with basil.

STEP 1

STEP 3

Cook's Notes

⏱ TIME: Preparation takes 10 minutes, cooking takes 20 minutes.

🄽 NUTRITIONAL DATA PER SERVING:
Calories   210
Protein   15g
Carbohydrates   35g
Fat   1g (5% of Calories)
Sodium   630mg

TURKEY AND BROWN RICE SOUP

Serves 8

A great use for turkey, this soup is a sure crowd pleaser. Its fresh taste makes a great first course for dinner or the perfect light lunch by itself.

2 cloves garlic, minced
3 cups (8oz) sliced fresh mushrooms
2 tbsps margarine
2 (14½oz) cans chicken broth
1 cup dry white wine
½ tsp dried thyme, crushed
¼ tsp ground black pepper
1 cup UNCLE BEN'S® Brand Fast Cooking Brown
    Rice – Ready in 10 Minutes
2 cups cubed cooked light turkey meat
⅔ cup finely chopped red bell pepper
½ cup green onion tops, diagonally cut into 1-inch
    pieces

1. In a large saucepan, sauté garlic and mushrooms in margarine for 1 minute.

STEP 1

2. Add chicken broth, wine, thyme, black pepper and rice. Bring to a boil, cover tightly, reduce heat and simmer for 10 minutes.

STEP 2

3. Stir in turkey and red bell pepper and heat thoroughly.

STEP 3

4. Garnish with green onion and serve.

Cook's Notes

🕐 TIME: Preparation takes 5 minutes, cooking takes 12 minutes.

Ⓝ NUTRITIONAL DATA PER SERVING:
Calories   170
Protein   14g
Carbohydrates   12g
Fat   5g (27% of Calories)
Sodium   390mg

STUFFED MUSHROOM HORS D'OEUVRES

Makes 24 mushrooms

These healthy hors d'oeuvres are prepared easily with the main course in the oven and provide an exciting beginning to any meal.

24 mushrooms 1½-2 inches in diameter
⅔ cup water
2 tbsps dry white wine
¼ cup finely chopped onion
¼ tsp dried savory, crushed
⅔ cup UNCLE BEN'S® Brand Rice In An Instant
1 tbsp margarine
¼ cup finely chopped green bell pepper
¼ cup finely chopped red bell pepper
3 tbsps grated Parmesan cheese
¼ cup unseasoned bread crumbs
Parsley sprigs to garnish

1. Preheat oven to 350°F.

2. Wash mushrooms, remove stems and chop enough of them to make 1 cup.

STEP 2

3. In a large saucepan, combine the water, wine, onion, mushroom stems and savory. Bring to a boil.

4. Stir in the rice, margarine, green bell pepper and red bell pepper. Cover, remove from heat and set aside until all liquid has been absorbed – about 5 minutes.

STEP 4

5. Stir in the Parmesan cheese and bread crumbs. Spoon the mixture into the centers of the mushroom caps.

STEP 5

6. Place the stuffed mushrooms in a lightly greased baking dish and bake in a 350°F oven for 18-20 minutes. Garnish each mushroom with a parsley sprig and serve.

Cook's Notes

⏱ TIME: Preparation takes 10-15 minutes, cooking takes 25 minutes.

ⓝ NUTRITIONAL DATA PER MUSHROOM:
Calories   25
Protein   1g
Carbohydrates   4g
Fat   less than 1g (27% of Calories)
Sodium   30mg

GINGERED SHRIMP AND VEGETABLE RICE

Serves 4

An elegant presentation for entertaining or a special meal for the family. This dish combines healthy eating and spicy oriental flavors with stir-fry convenience.

2⅔ cups water
1 cup UNCLE BEN'S® CONVERTED® Brand Rice
2½ tbsps reduced salt soy sauce
½lb fresh asparagus, cut into 1-inch pieces
½ cup diced red bell pepper
4 tsps vegetable oil
1lb medium shrimp, raw, peeled and deveined
4 cloves garlic, minced
1 tbsp grated fresh ginger root
¼ tsp dried red pepper flakes
½ cup dry white wine

---

1. In a medium saucepan, bring water to a boil. Stir in rice, cover tightly, reduce heat and simmer for 20 minutes.

STEP 2

2. Remove from heat, stir in soy sauce, asparagus and red bell pepper. Let stand, covered, while preparing shrimp.

3. Heat oil over medium-high heat in a non-stick skillet. Add shrimp, garlic, ginger and red pepper flakes. Stir-fry for 2 minutes.

STEP 3

4. Add wine and continue cooking until the shrimp are cooked through.

STEP 4

5. Spoon rice onto a serving plate and place the shrimp over the rice. Serve.

Cook's Notes

TIME: Preparation takes 10 minutes, cooking takes 30 minutes.

NUTRITIONAL DATA PER SERVING:
Calories   390
Protein   30g
Carbohydrates   45g
Fat   7g (18% of Calories)
Sodium   620mg

SOUTHWESTERN RICE

Serves 6

A quick and easy dish which is tasty too!

½ cup chopped onion
2 tsps vegetable oil
1 can (13¾ or 14½ ounces) beef broth
Water
1 cup frozen corn, thawed
1 tbsp minced jalapeño pepper
1 tsp Worcestershire sauce (optional)
¾ tsp ground cumin
2¼ cups UNCLE BEN'S® Brand Rice In An Instant
¼ cup thinly sliced ripe olives (optional)
2 tbsps chopped cilantro

STEP 3

3. Add the diluted broth, corn, jalapeño peppers, Worcestershire sauce, if desired, and cumin. Bring to a boil and stir in rice. Cover and remove from heat. Let stand 5 minutes, or until all liquid is absorbed.

4. Stir in olives, if desired. Sprinkle with cilantro and serve.

STEP 1

1. In a medium saucepan, cook onion in oil until tender.

2. Dilute broth with water to make 2¼ cups.

STEP 4

Cook's Notes

TIME: Preparation takes 5 minutes, cooking takes about 10 minutes.

NUTRITIONAL DATA PER SERVING:
Calories   170
Protein   5g
Carbohydrates   34g
Fat   2g (11% of Calories)
Sodium   250mg

SAGE BROWN RICE STUFFING

Serves 6

The savory blend of spices and brown rice makes this easy-to-prepare stuffing the perfect, healthy complement to any poultry dish.

2 tbsps margarine
1 cup chopped onion
1 cup chopped celery
¾ tsp rubbed dried sage
½ tsp poultry seasoning
⅛ tsp ground black pepper
1½ cups chicken broth
1¼ cups UNCLE BEN'S® Brand Fast Cooking
    Brown Rice – Ready in 10 Minutes
3 slices whole wheat bread, cut into ½-inch cubes

1. In a large saucepan, melt the margarine and sauté the onion and celery until tender – about 5 minutes.

2. Stir in sage, poultry seasoning and black pepper.

3. Add the chicken broth and rice. Bring to a boil, cover tightly, reduce heat and simmer for 10 minutes.

STEP 3

4. Remove from heat, stir in bread, cover and let stand for 5 minutes. Serve.

STEP 1

STEP 4

Cook's Notes

⏱ TIME: Preparation takes 10 minutes, cooking takes 20 minutes.

🄽 NUTRITIONAL DATA PER SERVING:
Calories   160
Protein   4g
Carbohydrates   25g
Fat   5g (29% of Calories)
Sodium   320mg

SOUTHERN PORK AND APPLE DINNER

Serves 4

Enjoy real southern hospitality with this savory and slightly sweet dish.

3 cups apple juice, divided
1 cup water
1 cup UNCLE BEN'S® CONVERTED® Brand Rice
¼ tsp salt
2 apples, with peel, chopped
2 tbsps flour
¼ tsp ground black pepper
½lb boneless pork loin, cut into thin strips
1 tbsp margarine
1 beef flavored bouillon cube
¼ cup finely chopped onion
Apple slices to garnish

1. In a medium saucepan, bring 1½ cups of apple juice and the water to a boil.

2. Stir in rice and salt. Cover tightly, reduce heat and simmer for 25 minutes, or until all liquid is absorbed. Stir in apple and set aside.

STEP 2

3. While rice is simmering, measure flour and pepper into a plastic bag. Shake pork strips in the bag until well coated with the flour and pepper.

STEP 3

4. Heat the margarine in a small skillet. Add the pork and cook over medium heat until pork is browned.

5. Add the remaining 1½ cups of apple juice, bouillon cube and onion to the skillet and stir. Cover and simmer over moderate heat until the sauce has a gravy-like consistency – about 20 minutes.

STEP 5

6. Spoon apple rice onto a serving dish and top with pork mixture. Serve garnished with the apple slices.

Cook's Notes

TIME: Preparation takes 10 minutes, cooking takes 30 minutes.

NUTRITIONAL DATA PER SERVING:

Calories   500
Protein   15g
Carbohydrates   74g
Fat   16g (29% of Calories)
Sodium   460mg

TURKEY RICE FAJITAS

Serves 4

Make dinner a social event with this healthy adaptation of a Tex-Mex favorite.

1 cup UNCLE BEN'S® Brand Fast Cooking Brown Rice – Ready in 10 Minutes
1¼ cups water
1 chicken flavored bouillon cube
1¼ tsps ground cumin
Dash ground red pepper
¼ tsp garlic powder, divided
2 tbsps margarine, divided
1 cup onion, halved and sliced
2 small red or green bell peppers, cut into thin strips
¼ tsp dried oregano, crushed
Dash black pepper
1½ cups cooked light turkey meat, cut into thin strips
1½ tbsps lime juice
2 tbsps plain lowfat yogurt
8 (8-inch) soft flour tortillas, warmed

1. In a medium saucepan, combine rice, water, bouillon cube, cumin, red pepper, half the garlic powder and half the margarine. Bring to a boil, cover, reduce heat and simmer for 10 minutes. Remove from heat and set aside until all water is absorbed – about 10 minutes.

2. While rice is simmering, melt remaining margarine in a 10-inch skillet. Add onion, bell peppers, oregano, black pepper and remaining garlic powder; sauté for 5 minutes. Stir in turkey and lime juice; heat through.

STEP 2

3. Stir yogurt into the rice and serve by spooning rice and turkey mixture onto warmed tortillas and fold. Serve two fajitas per person.

STEP 3

Cook's Notes

TIME: Preparation takes 20 minutes, cooking takes 15 minutes.

NUTRITIONAL DATA PER SERVING:
Calories 460
Protein 24g
Carbohydrates 65g
Fat 14g (26% of Calories)
Sodium 630mg

NEW ORLEANS FISH AND RICE CREOLE

Serves 4

Taste the flavor of old New Orleans in this healthy one-skillet dinner.

1lb flounder or sole fillets, skinned
½ tsp salt
1 (16oz) can whole tomatoes
Water
1 cup UNCLE BEN'S® CONVERTED® Brand Rice
1 cup coarsely chopped onion
4 garlic cloves, minced
2 tbsps lemon juice
2½ tsps dried basil, crushed
1 tsp dried oregano, crushed
½ tsp hot pepper sauce
¼ tsp ground black pepper
2 carrots, shredded
1 green bell pepper, cut into matchstick strips

---

1. Sprinkle fish fillets with salt, roll up skinned side in and secure with toothpicks. Set aside.

STEP 1

2. Drain and coarsely chop tomatoes, reserving liquid. Add enough water to the tomato juice to make 1⅓ cups.

3. In a large skillet, bring the tomato liquid to a boil and add tomatoes, rice, onion, garlic, lemon juice, basil, oregano, hot pepper sauce and black pepper. Arrange fish rolls on top of the rice. Return to a boil.

STEP 3

4. Cover tightly, reduce heat and simmer for 20 minutes.

5. Remove from heat and sprinkle carrot and green pepper over the fish. Cover again and let stand until all liquid is absorbed and fish flakes with a fork – about 5 minutes. Remove toothpicks from fish rolls before serving.

STEP 5

Cook's Notes

TIME: Preparation takes 15 minutes, cooking takes 30 minutes.

NUTRITIONAL DATA PER SERVING:
Calories   340
Protein   28g
Carbohydrates   54g
Fat   2g (6% of Calories)
Sodium   560mg

CONFETTI CHICKEN AND PEPPER RICE

Serves 4

Juicy chicken and pepper rice make a delicious flavor combination in this easy dish.

1½ cups chicken broth
½ cup <u>each</u> yellow, red, and green bell pepper
    strips (1 x ¼-inch)
1½ cups UNCLE BEN'S® Brand Rice In An Instant
1½ cups cubed cooked chicken breast or turkey
1 tbsp country style Dijon mustard
1 tsp honey
¼ cup thinly sliced green onions with tops

---

1. Bring broth and peppers to a boil in a saucepan.

2. Stir in rice, cover and remove from heat. Let stand 5 minutes, or until all liquid is absorbed.

STEP 2

STEP 4

STEP 1

3. While rice is standing, combine chicken, mustard, and honey.

4. Stir chicken mixture and green onions into rice and heat through.

Cook's Notes

🕐 TIME: Preparation takes 5 minutes, cooking takes about 10 minutes.

Ⓝ NUTRITIONAL DATA PER SERVING:
Calories   240
Protein   21g
Carbohydrates   32g
Fat   3g (11% of Calories)
Sodium   530mg

SHRIMP AND RICE VERACRUZ

Serves 6

Simplicity is the key to this seafood sensation. The perfect balance of tomatoes, green peppers, shrimp and long grain rice makes this an exciting dinner for your family.

1 (16oz) can whole tomatoes
Water
1 cup coarsely chopped onion
3 cloves garlic, minced
1 cup UNCLE BEN'S® CONVERTED® Brand Rice
2 bay leaves
½ cup (about 20) pimento stuffed green olives
¼ tsp salt
1lb shrimp, cooked and cleaned
1 large green pepper, cut into strips
Flat-leaved parsley to garnish

1. Drain and coarsely chop tomatoes, reserving juice. Add enough water to the juice to make 2½ cups.

STEP 1

2. In a skillet, combine tomato liquid, tomatoes, onion and garlic. Bring to a boil and stir in rice, bay leaves, olives and salt. Cover tightly, reduce heat and simmer for 20 minutes.

STEP 2

3. Stir in shrimp and green pepper. Remove from heat and let stand until all liquid is absorbed – about 10 minutes. Remove bay leaves and serve garnished with the parsley.

STEP 3

Cook's Notes

TIME: Preparation takes 5 minutes, cooking takes 30 minutes.

NUTRITIONAL DATA PER SERVING:
Calories   240
Protein   20g
Carbohydrates   32g
Fat   3g (13% of Calories)
Sodium   700mg

ITALIAN VEGETABLE RICE PIZZA

Serves 4

A pizza with pizzazz. The distinctive flavors of pizza accent the fresh vegetable toppings to make this a healthy meal and a family favorite.

1½ cups water
1½ cups UNCLE BEN'S® Brand Rice In An Instant
1½ cups (6oz) shredded part skim low moisture
    mozzarella cheese, divided
2 egg whites, slightly beaten
1 (8oz) can tomato sauce
¼ tsp dried basil, crushed
1 clove garlic, minced
¼ tsp dried oregano, crushed
½ small eggplant, sliced
½ cup thinly sliced zucchini
1 tomato, cut into thin wedges
2 tbsps grated Parmesan cheese
Fresh basil to garnish

STEP 3

1. Preheat oven to 400°F.

2. In a medium saucepan, bring water to a boil. Stir in rice, cover, remove from heat and set aside for 5 minutes, or until all liquid is absorbed.

3. Stir half the shredded mozzarella into the hot rice. When the cheese melts, stir in the beaten egg whites. Turn the mixture out onto a greased pizza pan and flatten to form a crust. Bake for 5 minutes in the 400°F oven.

4. Drizzle the tomato sauce over the crust and sprinkle with the basil, garlic and oregano. Arrange the eggplant, zucchini and tomato over the crust in a decorative pattern and top with the remaining mozzarella and the Parmesan cheese.

STEP 4

5. Bake near the top of the oven for 10 minutes, or until the vegetables are tender and the cheese is slightly browned. Garnish with fresh basil before serving.

Cook's Notes

TIME: Preparation takes 10 minutes, cooking takes 20 minutes.

NUTRITIONAL DATA PER SERVING:
Calories   290
Protein   18g
Carbohydrates   35g
Fat   8g (26% of Calories)
Sodium   660mg

EASY SUMMER RICE SALAD

Serves 8

This cool, crunchy salad with a soy-ginger vinaigrette dressing is a natural for a summer afternoon luncheon. So easy to prepare you will want to serve it year round.

2 tbsps sherry
1 tbsp reduced salt soy sauce
¼ tsp sesame oil
¼ tsp grated fresh ginger root
4 tbsps cider vinegar
3 tbsps vegetable oil
1 tbsp Dijon mustard
1 clove garlic, minced
2¼ cups water
2¼ cups UNCLE BEN'S® Brand Rice In An Instant
1 (10oz) package frozen peas, thawed
½ cup sliced green onions
1½ cups cubed cooked light chicken meat
½ cup diced celery
2 tbsps diced green bell pepper
2 tbsps diced red bell pepper

STEP 1

3. In a large bowl, combine the rice, peas, onion, chicken, celery, green and red bell peppers and toss. Pour salad dressing over the mixture and toss again.

1. To make salad dressing, combine sherry, soy sauce, sesame oil, ginger, vinegar, vegetable oil, mustard and garlic in a jar. Shake well.

2. In a large saucepan, bring water to a boil. Stir in rice, cover, remove from heat and set aside for 5 minutes, or until all liquid is absorbed.

STEP 3

4. Spoon into a serving dish, cover and chill for ½ hour before serving.

Cook's Notes

⌐ TIME: Preparation takes 10 minutes.

ⁿ NUTRITIONAL DATA PER SERVING:
Calories   220
Protein   12g
Carbohydrates   29g
Fat   7g (27% of Calories)
Sodium   190mg

GARDEN VEGETABLE BROWN RICE

Serves 6

The simplicity of this recipe allows you to enjoy brown rice at its best. The vegetables complement the brown rice to give you a nutritious and flavorful side dish.

2 tsps margarine
1 clove garlic, minced
2⅔ cups water
½ tsp salt
¼ tsp ground nutmeg
1 cup UNCLE BEN'S® Brand Original Whole Grain Brown Rice
2 cups fresh broccoli florets
3 cups (8oz) sliced fresh mushrooms
1 cup halved cherry tomatoes
¾ cup (3oz) shredded part skim low moisture mozzarella cheese

1. In a large skillet, melt margarine and sauté garlic for 2 minutes.

2. Add water, salt, and nutmeg. Bring to a boil and add rice. Cover tightly, reduce heat and simmer for 40 minutes.

3. Top with broccoli and mushrooms, cover, and simmer for 10 more minutes.

STEP 3

4. Stir in cherry tomato halves and heat through. Sprinkle with cheese and serve.

STEP 2

STEP 4

Cook's Notes

TIME: Preparation takes 5 minutes, cooking takes 55 minutes.

NUTRITIONAL DATA PER SERVING:
Calories   190
Protein   9g
Carbohydrates   30g
Fat   5g (22% of Calories)
Sodium   280mg

ROSEMARY CHICKEN STIR-FRY

Serves 4

Healthy, attractive and, best of all, easy – this dish is a quick solution for dinner any day of the week.

1 quart water
1 UNCLE BEN'S® Brand Rice Boil-in-Bag Family Serving Size
1½ tbsps vegetable oil
1 cup carrots, cut into matchstick strips
½ cup sliced celery
¼ tsp dried rosemary, crushed
½lb chicken breasts, boned, skinned, cut into thin strips
1 cup (3oz) sliced fresh mushrooms
¼ cup sliced green onions
1 (10¾oz) can condensed chicken broth
4 tsps cornstarch
Fresh rosemary to garnish

STEP 3

4. Add mushrooms and green onions, and stir-fry another 3 minutes.

5. Stir broth and cornstarch together in a small bowl until smooth, then stir into the skillet.

STEP 5

1. In a large saucepan, bring 1 quart of water to a boil. Completely submerge the unopened bag of rice in the water. Boil gently, uncovered, for 10 minutes. Remove bag, drain and cut open. Empty onto a serving dish.

2. While rice is cooking, heat oil in a large skillet over medium-high heat and stir-fry carrots, celery and rosemary until the vegetables are tender-crisp.

3. Push the vegetables to one side and add chicken. Stir-fry chicken for 3 minutes or until it is no longer pink.

6. Cook over medium heat until the mixture thickens, stirring often.

7. Serve the chicken mixture over the rice and garnish with fresh rosemary.

Cook's Notes

⌂ TIME: Preparation takes 10 minutes, cooking takes 10 minutes.

Ⓝ NUTRITIONAL DATA PER SERVING:
Calories   250
Protein   19g
Carbohydrates   28g
Fat   7g (25% of Calories)
Sodium   550mg

FESTIVE CHICKEN SHISH KEBABS WITH RICE

Serves 6

Add excitement to your next meal with this striking combination of chicken-vegetable kebabs on a delightful bed of herbed rice.

1 tsp ground paprika
1 cup dry white wine
2 tbsps vegetable oil
1 tsp dried rosemary, crushed
2 cloves garlic, minced
1lb chicken breasts, skinned and cut into 1½-inch cubes
1 medium zucchini, cut in ½-inch slices
1 large red pepper, cut in 1½-inch squares
1 large yellow pepper, cut into 1½-inch squares
1 (14½oz) can chicken broth
1 cup UNCLE BEN'S® CONVERTED® Brand Rice
2 tbsps chopped green onions
Watercress to garnish

STEP 2

STEP 4

1. Combine paprika, wine, oil, rosemary and garlic in a large bowl. Stir to mix, then add chicken cubes and marinate for 30 minutes.

2. After marinating, alternately thread the chicken, zucchini and red and yellow bell peppers onto skewers. Reserve marinade.

3. Preheat broiler.

4. Pour the marinade into a medium saucepan, reserving 3 tablespoons. Add the chicken broth and rice. Bring mixture to a boil, cover tightly, reduce heat and simmer for 20 minutes. Stir in green onions and set aside until all liquid is absorbed – about 5 minutes.

5. While the rice is cooking, broil the skewers about 4 to 5-inches from the heat source for 8-10 minutes. Brush just before broiling with the reserved marinade. Turn once during cooking and brush with marinade again.

6. Arrange kebabs over rice and serve garnished with watercress.

Cook's Notes

TIME: Preparation takes 15 minutes, marinating takes 30 minutes and cooking takes 35 minutes.

NUTRITIONAL DATA PER SERVING:
Calories   290
Protein   22g
Carbohydrates   29g
Fat   6g (20% of Calories)
Sodium   270mg

MOROCCAN CHICKEN AND RICE

Serves 4

The unique combination of ingredients in this recipe takes ordinary chicken and creates an exciting meal with an international flavor your family will enjoy.

---

4 chicken breast halves (1lb), boned and skinned
1 tbsp margarine
1 (10¾oz) can condensed chicken broth
Water
1 cup UNCLE BEN'S® CONVERTED® Brand Rice
¼ tsp ground black pepper
¼ tsp ground cinnamon
¼ tsp ground allspice
½ cup dried currants
¼ cup sliced green onions
2½ tbsps orange liqueur
1½ tsps grated orange peel
¼ cup slivered almonds
Fresh mint leaves for garnish

---

1. In a skillet, brown the chicken breasts in margarine, cooking about 2-3 minutes per side. Remove the chicken breasts from the pan and set aside.

2. Dilute broth with water to make 2½ cups.

3. Add the diluted broth to the skillet. Stir in rice, black pepper, cinnamon and allspice, and bring to a boil. Cover tightly, reduce heat and simmer for 10 minutes.

STEP 3

4. Stir in the currants, green onions, orange liqueur and orange peel. Lay the chicken breasts on top of the rice. Return to a simmer, cover and simmer for another 10 minutes.

STEP 4

5. Remove from heat and set aside until all liquid is absorbed – about 5 minutes. Top the rice and chicken with almonds and serve garnished with fresh mint.

Cook's Notes

⏱ TIME: Preparation takes 10 minutes, cooking takes 30 minutes.

𝐧 NUTRITIONAL DATA PER SERVING:
Calories   490
Protein   36g
Carbohydrates   59g
Fat   10g (19% of Calories)
Sodium   590mg

CHILI CON CARNE

Serves 6

This unique recipe can handle a Texas-size appetite and still be a part of today's healthy lifestyle.

½lb lean ground beef
1 cup chopped onion
1 (16oz) can kidney beans, undrained
1 (6oz) can tomato paste
2½ tsps chili powder
½ tsp ground cumin
2 cups water
¾ cup UNCLE BEN'S® CONVERTED® Brand Rice
¼ tsp salt
½ tsp finely chopped jalapeño pepper
1 medium tomato, chopped
½ cup shredded cheddar cheese
Flat-leaved parsley to garnish
Tortilla chips (optional)

1. In a large skillet, brown ground beef and onions. Drain fat.

2. Add the beans with liquid, tomato paste, chili powder, cumin, water, rice, salt, jalapeño and tomato. Stir well. Bring to a boil, cover, reduce heat and simmer for 25 minutes.

STEP 2

3. Garnish with cheese and parsley, and serve with tortilla chips.

STEP 1

STEP 3

Cook's Notes

TIME: Preparation takes 5 minutes, cooking takes 30 minutes.

NUTRITIONAL DATA PER SERVING:
Calories   330
Protein   19g
Carbohydrates   40g
Fat   11g (30% of Calories)
Sodium   680mg

ORIENTAL BROWN RICE SALAD

Serves 8

Unlock the secrets of healthy oriental cooking with this spicy brown rice salad. Serve with chicken, fish or beef.

---

2 tbsps vegetable oil
2 tsps sesame oil
3 tbsps cider vinegar
3 tbsps reduced salt soy sauce
2 tsps grated fresh ginger root
1 clove garlic, minced
⅛ tsp ground red pepper
2 tbsps sesame seeds
3 cups water
2½ cups UNCLE BEN'S® Brand Fast Cooking
    Brown Rice – Ready in 10 Minutes
1 cup shredded carrot
1 green bell pepper, cut into thin strips
2 medium tomatoes, chopped
1 cup snow peas, cut in half
½ cup sliced water chestnuts

---

1. To make salad dressing, combine the vegetable oil, sesame oil, vinegar, soy sauce, ginger, garlic, red pepper and sesame seeds in a jar. Shake well.

2. In a large saucepan, bring the water to a boil. Stir in the rice, cover, reduce heat and simmer for 10 minutes. Remove from heat and chill rice until cool – about 1 hour.

STEP 2

3. In a bowl stir the carrot, bell pepper, tomatoes, snow peas and water chestnuts together with the chilled rice. Pour the salad dressing over the mixture and toss well. Serve.

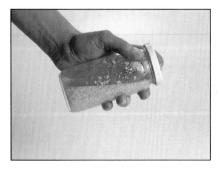

STEP 1

STEP 3

Cook's Notes

🕒 TIME: Preparation takes 5 minutes, cooking takes 10 minutes and chilling takes 1 hour.

ⓝ NUTRITIONAL DATA PER SERVING:
Calories   190
Protein   4g
Carbohydrates   30g
Fat   7g (30% of Calories)
Sodium   290mg

TEX-MEX SUNBURST

Serves 4

This festive south of the border treat will add spice to your menu. Great for casual entertaining or a healthy family meal.

---

5 (6-inch) corn tortillas
1 (16oz) can no salt added whole tomatoes
½lb lean ground beef
½ cup chopped onion
1 quart water
1 UNCLE BEN'S® Brand Rice Boil-in-Bag
   Family Serving Size
1 (15½oz) can kidney beans, drained
3 tbsps no salt added tomato paste
1 tbsp chopped jalapeño pepper
1 tbsp chili powder
1 tsp ground cumin
¼ tsp salt
¼ tsp ground red pepper
½ cup (2oz) shredded Monterey Jack cheese
2 tbsps chopped cilantro (optional)

---

1. Preheat oven to 400°F.

2. Cut each tortilla into 8 wedges and arrange in a

single layer on a cookie sheet. Bake at 400°F for 5-10 minutes until the wedges are crisp. Set aside.

3. Drain tomatoes, reserving juice. Chop coarsely and set aside.

4. In a large skillet, brown ground beef and onion. Drain off the fat.

5. In a large saucepan, bring 1 quart of water to a boil. Completely submerge the unopened bag of rice in the water. Boil gently, uncovered, for 10 minutes. Remove bag, drain and cut open. Empty the rice onto the center of a serving dish.

6. While rice is cooking, add to beef and onion in skillet: beans, tomatoes and their juice, tomato paste, jalapeño, chili powder, cumin, salt and red pepper. Mix well and bring to a boil. Reduce heat and simmer for 10 minutes, or until the mixture thickens.

STEP 6

STEP 2

7. Top the rice with the beef mixture and arrange the tortilla chips around the outside edge of the serving dish. Sprinkle cheese and cilantro over the top and serve.

Cook's Notes

TIME: Preparation takes 15 minutes, cooking takes 30 minutes.

NUTRITIONAL DATA PER SERVING:
Calories   520
Protein   30g
Carbohydrates   64g
Fat   18g (30% of Calories)
Sodium   710mg

HARVEST FRUIT BROWN RICE

Serves 6

This delicious medley of fruit, almonds and brown rice will soon become one of your all-time favorite recipes.

2⅔ cups water
1 cup UNCLE BEN'S® Brand Original Whole Grain
   Brown Rice
1 cup peeled and chopped apple
¼ cup chopped onion
½ tsp salt
1 tbsp margarine
½ cup slivered almonds
½ cup dried apricots, chopped
2 tbsps honey
Fresh mint to garnish

1. In a large saucepan, bring water to a boil. Stir in rice, apple, onion and salt. Return mixture to a boil, cover tightly, reduce heat and simmer for 50 minutes.

2. In a small skillet, melt margarine and lightly brown the almonds.

STEP 2

3. Stir almond and margarine mixture, apricots and honey into the hot rice. Serve garnished with the fresh mint.

STEP 1

STEP 3

Cook's Notes

TIME: Preparation takes 5 minutes, cooking takes 50 minutes.

NUTRITIONAL DATA PER SERVING:
Calories   260
Protein   6g
Carbohydrates   43g
Fat   9g (29% of Calories)
Sodium   200mg

HEARTY SAUSAGE AND BROWN RICE BAKE

Serves 6

A complete meal on its own. The hearty flavor creates a casserole that will spice up any evening.

Non-stick cooking spray
½lb turkey breakfast sausage
1 cup sliced celery
1 cup chopped onion
1 (16oz) can no salt added whole tomatoes
1½ cups UNCLE BEN'S® Brand Fast Cooking Brown Rice – Ready in 10 Minutes
1 (15oz) can kidney beans, undrained
1 cup water
2 tsps dried oregano, crushed
1 tsp garlic powder
½ tsp ground black pepper
½ tsp dried basil, crushed
¼ tsp ground red pepper
½ cup (2oz) shredded cheddar cheese
Fresh oregano to garnish

1. Preheat oven to 350°F.

2. Spray an unheated large skillet with non-stick cooking spray. Add the sausage, celery and onion, and cook over medium heat until the sausage browns.

3. Drain tomatoes, reserving juice. Chop coarsely and set aside.

4. Combine the sausage mixture, rice, kidney beans, tomatoes and their juice, water, oregano, garlic powder, black pepper, basil, and red pepper in a 2½ quart casserole dish. Mix well.

5. Bake, uncovered, at 350°F for 25 minutes.

STEP 4

6. Sprinkle with cheese and bake until the cheese melts. Serve garnished with the oregano.

STEP 6

Cook's Notes

⏱ TIME: Preparation takes 10 minutes, cooking takes 30-35 minutes.

🅽 NUTRITIONAL DATA PER SERVING:
Calories   300
Protein   17g
Carbohydrates   36g
Fat   10g (29% of Calories)
Sodium   590mg

WALDORF RICE SALAD

Serves 4

A guaranteed success. This recipe needs no watching to prepare. Delicious as a side dish or a healthy snack.

1½ cups apple juice
1¼ cups UNCLE BEN'S® Brand Rice In An Instant
⅛ tsp salt
Dash cinnamon
Dash nutmeg
⅔ cup chopped red apple, with peel
⅓ cup sliced celery
¼ cup chopped walnuts
3 tbsps lowfat yogurt
Celery leaves to garnish

Cover, remove from heat and chill until rice is cool – about 1 hour.

STEP 1

2. Stir in apple, celery, walnuts, and yogurt. Transfer to a serving bowl and serve garnished with the celery leaves.

Chopping the apple and celery

1. In a medium saucepan, heat apple juice to a boil. Stir in rice, salt, cinnamon, and nutmeg.

STEP 2

Cook's Notes

TIME: Preparation takes 5 minutes, cooking takes 1 minute and chilling takes 1 hour.

NUTRITIONAL DATA PER SERVING:
Calories   210
Protein   4g
Carbohydrates   38g
Fat   5g (22% of Calories)
Sodium   95mg

GREEK LEMON AND DILL RICE

Serves 4

Rediscover an ancient Greek flavor combination. The refreshing flavors of lemon and dill make this dish a perfect accompaniment for chicken or fish.

1 (14½oz) can chicken broth
Water
2 tbsps fresh lemon juice
1 cup UNCLE BEN'S® CONVERTED® Brand Rice
¼ cup sliced green onions
1 tsp dried dill weed
1 tsp grated lemon peel
⅛ tsp ground black pepper
Lemon slices and fresh dill to garnish

1. Dilute broth with water to make 2½ cups.

2. Pour diluted broth into a medium saucepan, add lemon juice and bring to a boil. Stir in rice, cover tightly, reduce heat and simmer for 20 minutes.

3. Remove from heat and let stand, covered, until all liquid is absorbed – about 5 minutes.

STEP 3

4. Stir in green onions, dill, lemon peel and black pepper. Serve garnished with lemon slices and fresh dill.

STEP 2

STEP 4

Cook's Notes

t. TIME: Preparation takes 5 minutes, cooking takes 30 minutes.

n NUTRITIONAL DATA PER SERVING:
Calories   190
Protein   6g
Carbohydrates   40g
Fat   1g (5% of Calories)
Sodium   330mg

AUTHENTIC NORTH INDIAN CURRY

Serves 8

This exotic blend of spices can only be found in the most authentic curries, and will transform an ordinary meal into an Indian feast.

2 tbsps vegetable oil
½ tsp cumin seeds
6 whole cloves
2 (1-inch long) cinnamon sticks
½ tsp grated fresh ginger root
2 cloves garlic, minced
½ tsp ground turmeric
½ tsp ground coriander
1 tsp ground cumin
¼ tsp ground red pepper (½ tsp if you like it HOT!)
1 tsp salt
3 cups water
1½ cups UNCLE BEN'S® CONVERTED® Brand Rice
½ cup sliced green beans
½ cup frozen peas, thawed
¼ cup shredded carrots

STEP 2

3. Add water and rice, bring to a boil, cover tightly, reduce heat and simmer for 20 minutes.

STEP 3

1. In a large saucepan, heat the oil over medium-high heat. Add cumin seeds and allow them to fry in the oil for a few seconds until they crackle.

2. Add the cloves, cinnamon sticks, ginger, and garlic and sauté for a few seconds. Add turmeric, coriander, ground cumin, red pepper and salt. Mix well.

4. Remove from heat and stir in green beans, peas and carrots. Cover and set aside until all liquid is absorbed – about 5 minutes. Serve.

Cook's Notes

TIME: Preparation takes 5 minutes, cooking takes about 20 minutes.

NUTRITIONAL DATA PER SERVING:
Calories   170
Protein   4g
Carbohydrates   31g
Fat   4g (20% of Calories)
Sodium   280mg

TODAY'S RICE PUDDING

Serves 5

Makes a great dessert without making you feel guilty. A perfect ending to any meal.

⅓ cup UNCLE BEN'S® CONVERTED® Brand Rice
1½ cups water
¼ cup sugar
1 tsp cornstarch
¼ tsp salt
1⅓ cups skim milk
2 tsps margarine
1 tsp vanilla
2 egg yolks, beaten
Ground cinnamon (optional)

STEP 4

3. Remove from heat, and stir in margarine and vanilla.

4. Slowly stir about 1 cup of hot rice mixture into beaten egg yolks; blend with remaining mixture in saucepan.

5. Cook over medium heat, stirring frequently until pudding starts to bubble.

6. Serve warm or chilled. If desired, garnish with cinnamon.

STEP 2

1. In a medium saucepan, bring rice and water to a boil. Cover tightly and simmer for 25 minutes, or until rice is very tender and most of water is absorbed.

2. Combine sugar, cornstarch and salt in a bowl. Stir in milk and blend well. Add to rice and bring to boil. Boil 1 minute, stirring constantly.

STEP 5

Cook's Notes

🕐 TIME: Cooking takes about 35 minutes.

ⓝ NUTRITIONAL DATA PER SERVING:
Calories   150
Protein   4g
Carbohydrates   24g
Fat   4g (24% of Calories)
Sodium   160mg

BROWN RICE APPLE CRISP

Serves 8

Try this recipe once and your family will be hooked. A classic apple crisp with a healthy new twist. Excellent alone or with a scoop of vanilla ice cream.

1¼ cups water
1 cup UNCLE BEN'S® Brand Fast Cooking Brown
    Rice – Ready in 10 Minutes
3½ cups peeled and sliced cooking apples
1 tbsp lemon juice
½ tsp cinnamon
¼ tsp salt
1 cup brown sugar, packed, divided
¾ cup flour
5 tbsps margarine
¼ cup chopped walnuts

1. Preheat oven to 350°F.

2. In a medium saucepan, bring water to a boil. Stir in rice, reduce heat, cover tightly and simmer for 10 minutes. Remove from heat and set aside until all liquid is absorbed – about 5 minutes.

STEP 2

3. Combine rice, apples, lemon juice, cinnamon, salt and half the brown sugar. Spread into a greased 8-inch round baking dish.

STEP 3

4. Cut flour, remaining brown sugar, and margarine together until the mixture is uniformly crumbly. Stir in walnuts and sprinkle mixture over the apples and rice.

STEP 4

5. Bake in a 350°F oven for 30 minutes. Serve.

Cook's Notes

TIME: Preparation takes 15 minutes, cooking takes 40 minutes.

NUTRITIONAL DATA PER SERVING:
Calories   300
Protein   3g
Carbohydrates   52g
Fat   10g (29% of Calories)
Sodium   170mg

RASPBERRY YOGURT PARFAITS

Serves 8

No one will ever guess this dessert is so easy to prepare and healthy too. Perfect for a special occasion or a healthy after school treat for the kids.

¾ cup water
¾ cup UNCLE BEN'S® Brand Rice In An Instant
2 (8oz) cartons raspberry lowfat yogurt
2 cups fresh raspberries
Fresh mint leaves to garnish

STEP 2

1. In a small saucepan, bring water to a boil. Stir in rice, cover, remove from heat and set aside for 5 minutes, or until all liquid is absorbed.

3. Just before serving, layer rice mixture and berries in parfait glasses or dessert dishes and garnish with fresh mint leaves.

STEP 1

2. Cool rice to room temperature, stir in yogurt and chill for 30 minutes.

STEP 3

Cook's Notes

⏱ TIME: Preparation takes 10 minutes, chilling takes 30 minutes.

❓ VARIATION: Mix and match your favorite fresh fruits with your favorite fruit flavored yogurts.

⋂ NUTRITIONAL DATA PER SERVING:
Calories   100
Protein   3g
Carbohydrates   21g
Fat   less than 1g (7% of Calories)
Sodium   35mg

PEACHY RICE DESSERT
Serves 8

Kids and adults alike will enjoy this delicious dessert.

2 quarts water
2 UNCLE BEN'S® Brand Rice Boil-in-Bags Family
   Serving Size
1 package (3½ ounces) vanilla instant pudding and
   pie filling mix
2¼ cups skim milk
1 carton (8 ounces) vanilla low-fat yogurt
½ tsp almond extract
3 fresh peaches, peeled and thinly sliced*
1 tbsp toasted sliced almonds (optional)

1. In a large saucepan, bring 2 quarts of water to a boil. Completely submerge the unopened bags of rice in the water. Boil gently, uncovered, for 10 minutes. Remove bags, drain and cut open. Empty into a large bowl and cool rice to room temperature.

STEP 2

2. Prepare pudding according to package directions, using 2¼ cups skim milk. Stir in rice, yogurt and almond extract.

3. Layer rice mixture and peaches in 8 dessert glasses beginning and ending with rice mixture.

4. Cover and chill; garnish with sliced almonds, if desired.

STEP 1

STEP 3

Cook's Notes

TIME: Preparation and cooking takes about 25 minutes.

? VARIATION: *One package (about 12 onces) frozen unsweetened sliced peaches, thawed and drained, or 1 can (15 or 16 ounces) sliced peaches packed in juice, drained, may be substituted.

n NUTRITIONAL DATA PER SERVING:
Calories   210
Protein   6g
Carbohydrates   44g
Fat   Less than 1g (3% of Calories)
Sodium   250mg

INDEX

Photography by Peter Barry
Recipes prepared and styled by Helen Burdett
Designed by Judith Chant
Edited by Jillian Stewart
Project co-ordination by Hanni Penrose